BREEDERS' BEST
A KENNEL CLUB BOOK

Maltese

By Anna Katherine Nic[...]

D1542676

BREEDERS' BEST
A KENNEL CLUB BOOK

MALTESE

ISBN: 1-59378-928-9

Copyright © 2004

Kennel Club Books, LLC
308 Main Street, Allenhurst, NJ 07711 USA
Printed in South Korea

PHOTOS BY:
Paulette Braun, Bernd Brinkmann, Isabelle Français, Greta Franklin and Carol Ann Johnson.

DRAWINGS BY:
Yolyanko el Habanero.

Contents

Meet the Maltese

A model of a dog dating back to around 8000 BC is believed to have been a child's toy and, yes, you've guessed, the dog is believed to be a Maltese! If you love dolls, you will love the Maltese, because it likes to be treated rather like a precious doll and adores being the baby of his human family. The more attention you give it, the happier the Maltese will be.

Those who have an interest in the history of Rome will be interested in

The Maltese has been a favored pet for thousands of years. Fanciers throughout the ages have been attracted to the breed's flowing white coat and delicate beauty.

knowing that Emperor Claudius had a dog like this himself, and it is very probable that the Romans took dogs of Maltese type to Asia. They finally arrived in China, where they likely became romantically entangled with those alluring lionesses we know as Pekingese.

Maltese might just be the world's cutest puppies. It's no wonder why, for many, it's love at first sight with this breed.

It is not always easy to establish exactly which dogs were which when looking at very old images, for several types had their coats styled into the "lion trim." So here is perhaps the place to clarify that not every old picture we see of a dog with this haircut is a Löwchen (as many breed enthusiasts would wish); some of them were probably Maltese. The Löwchen is a small German breed that is sometimes called the "Little Lion Dog." In fact, the Maltese has been known by several different names over the centuries, "Maltese Lion Dog" being one of interest here.

The Maltese is well established and enjoys great popularity the world over. Beautiful Maltese can be found in many countries, like this lovely example from Germany.

Other names have included "Ye Ancient Dogge of Malta," "Comforter," "Spaniel Gentle" and "Shock Dog."

From pre-Christian times, it is not at all unusual to find that some objects feature images of the breed, while in Imperial Rome it was called the "Roman Ladies"; then the breed was a great favorite with the ladies, as indeed it still is today. Maltese were closely involved with Egyptian culture, especially between 600 and 300 BC, when they were worshiped, much like royal family members.

In ancient Greece, Aristotle wrote of the breed in about 350 BC, but images of these dogs have been found on Greek vases a century or so older than that. If you are familiar with Italian art, you may have noticed that many Renaissance and pre-Raphaelite painters included Maltese-like dogs in their works of art.

So it is evident that there is geographical confusion regarding the actual origin of the Maltese, exacerbated by the fact that there used to be a town called Melitia in Sicily, where dogs called *Canis Melitei* were found. Aristotle believed the breed came from Malta, and to further add to the confusion, Malta was earlier known as the Island of Melita.

A prominent canine writer in the 19th century wrote that the Maltese was found not only in Malta but also on other Mediterranean islands, where they were affectionate to their owners but apparently ill-tempered toward strangers. Yet another theory about the origin of the breed is that it was one of the original French toy breeds. Indeed there is no disputing the fact that the Maltese is certainly a close relation of the bichon dogs, including the Bichon Frisé, Coton de

The Maltese has long been connected with being the pampered dogs of royalty, and many Maltese today sit upon the thrones in their families.

Tulear, Bolognese and Havanese. Some have even thought that the Maltese hailed from the Gobi desert, this on account of the breed's love of sun and heat.

Undoubtedly the Maltese found its way around the world with traders of one kind or another and was often bartered, frequently for Chinese silk, a commodity so precious that it was worth its weight in gold. Sometimes the dogs were taken to the shore to be sold, but sometimes boat owners simply offered their silken pups to the passengers for sale.

Although the breed has sometimes been called the

The Bichon Frisé is the most well-known of the Maltese's relatives.

Maltese Terrier, it is by no means a traditional "go-to-ground" terrier. Perhaps the word "terrier" found its way into the name because the Maltese was able to catch

You'd be hard pressed today to find a Maltese who could make his living as a working farm terrier.

In 1650 a German physician wrote about the

Another of the bichon breeds, the Bolognese, originally hails from Italy.

small rodents. Indeed, in maritime cities of the Mediterranean, Maltese were renowned for hunting mice and rats in harbor warehouses and ships' holds.

breed, describing it as the size of a wood weasel. Interestingly, he mentioned that there were black and white ones and red and white ones, the latter most valued.

To keep them small, Maltese sadly were kept in tiny baskets. In these they were fed the very choicest food, and their beds were lined with beautiful fleeces. It is not actually known when the breed first appeared in the Romans, but some maintain that it did not arrive until the reign of King Henry VIII. Indeed the breed was in great demand in Britain during the 19th century. In 1859, a little white bitch called Psyche

The Havanese is Cuba's delightful contribution to the bichon family of dogs.

Germany, but it was certainly there during the 19th century, and in 1900 a stud book was commenced.

It is likely that the Maltese came to Britain with was rather cutely described as looking like "a ball of animated floss!" She weighed about 3 pounds and her coat was 15 inches long. This was a convenient little breed for hawkers to sell in the streets, and when a dog had staining on his face, the sellers said these were tear stains from weeping! How gullible were the purchasers of the day, nearly as uninformed as many dog owners today who believe that the "doggy in the window" is supposed to have cloudy eyes or a matted coat. I suppose this was similar to the selling techniques employed by some less reputable market-traders today—but they were selling dogs, not fruit! Our dogs are supposed to last longer than a week without refrigeration!

As the trend for tiny Toys grew, people wanted to breed the Maltese smaller and smaller. In doing so, however, they made them difficult to breed, and they were lacking in vitality. Larger dogs were introduced to Britain from the

All bichon breeds have magnificent coats, aptly illustrated by the Maltese's long white locks.

Continent, so eventually the breed returned to its more normal weight of 4–9 pounds.

Owners who exhibited their Maltese in the 19th century kept the dogs' hind feet in bags made of wash-leather to stop them from scratching and damaging their skin. Unfortunately, when worn for long periods of time, these actually damaged the feet, for the temperature was too hot!

Some dedicated owners plaited their dogs' hair, even in those days. Plaiting is a method of wrapping the coat to avoid breakage. The dogs' diet was also very carefully attended to, so we can see that the Maltese as a companion dog was very highly rated. However, it did have the reputation for being a little snappy, so many who admired the Maltese for its beauty chose not to own the breed.

The Maltese still had its followers in Britain at the beginning of the 20th century but, during World War I (1914–1918), breeding was curtailed and the Maltese Club of London disbanded. It was believed that there were no Maltese left at all on the island of Malta, but a few were imported from the Continent and the breed was revived. By 1934, the Maltese Club had been founded, and since then the breed has become one of the more popular breeds in the English Kennel Club's Toy Group.

In the US, the American Kennel Club (AKC) accepted the breed in 1888, but it had been shown before then in

At the top of the toys, the Maltese, with his glistening white coat and sparkling dark eyes, has captured hearts around the world.

the AKC's Miscellaneous Class, under the name Maltese Lion Dog. In fact, at the very first Westminster Kennel Club dog show, the most prestigious show in America, a Maltese competed. The breed gained in popularity and, during the years of World War I, almost 200 were registered, with several breeders becoming prominent once the war was over. Sadly, during World War II there was a serious decline in numbers, but the breed did indeed survive. As the years went by, new blood was introduced from abroad. The American Maltese Association was founded in 1961, and its first National Specialty was held on Valentine's Day in 1971. The Maltese had most certainly captured a good many hearts by then! Today the Maltese is one of the most popular Toy dogs registered by the AKC and surely counts among the most accomplished show dogs in the ring.

MEET THE MALTESE

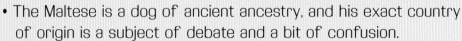

Overview

- The Maltese is a dog of ancient ancestry, and his exact country of origin is a subject of debate and a bit of confusion.
- The Maltese is one of the bichon breeds, a group of small companion dogs known for their beautiful coats.
- The Maltese has been known around the world for centuries, having spread to different countries as it traveled with traders.
- The Maltese has long had the reputation of being a pampered pet, highly prized by fanciers.
- The Maltese is a Toy breed and is one of the most popular in the group in both the US and UK.

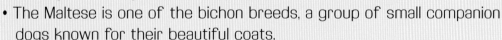

Description of the Maltese

The Maltese is a toy dog, a lively, intelligent little pet that is very alert. His sweet-tempered nature, coupled with his smart long white coat of silky hair and his proud head carriage, makes him thoroughly endearing to devotees of the breed. In the adult, the hair falls to the ground and the plumed tail is carried gracefully over the back. The Maltese has no undercoat, but is a single-coated breed. The headfall is tied up in a topknot, or often in two, depending on the country. All in all,

The Maltese's sweet temperament and small size make him an ideal pet for owners of all ages, activity levels and living situations—as long as the owners have plenty of love to give!

the Maltese is a highly eye-catching dog and makes a very pretty picture indeed.

This is a well-balanced dog, essentially short and cobby, with good spring of rib and a level back from withers to tail. Legs are short, but the shoulders are well sloped and the hind legs well angulated. If the forelegs are straight, these features combine to make for straight, free-flowing movement, without any weaving of the legs in and out as the dogs moves toward you.

Although the coat of the Maltese is perhaps considered his crowning glory, there can be no denying that the head and expression are thoroughly endearing. There is equal balance from the stop to the tip of the nose and from the stop to the center of the skull. The stop, which is the indentation between the eyes where the skull meets the nasal bone, is well defined. The Maltese does not have a

The crowning glory of the Maltese is undoubtedly its full-length silky coat of pure white.

The Maltese has an impressive headfall, and the black pigmentation and dark eyes create a striking contrast against the solid white coat.

snipy muzzle; instead, it is broad and well filled under the eye.

The nose should be true black, in keeping with the pads of the rounded feet. The black nose is matched by the black pigment on the eye rims, which surround a

The Maltese has a regular, complete scissors bite, meaning that the upper teeth closely overlap the lower; a level or edge-to-edge bite is also seen in the breed. The edges of the lips are to be absolutely black.

The color of the Maltese is

Many companion Maltese are kept in a cute low-maintenance clip known as a pet trim. This dog's haircut is dressed up with a fun bandana.

round, dark brown eye that does not bulge. The eyes are round and very dark, again with black eye rims.

pure white, but tinges of color also appear in some dogs, though what is permissible and what is not differs slightly according to the country and the breed standard in use. Light lemon or tan markings are seen but are not desirable in a show dog. The coat should be pure white, but a pale ivory tinge should not be considered undesirable. According to the European breed standard, "Traces of pale orange shades are tolerated but not desirable and constitute an imperfection."

Lastly we come to height, which should not exceed 10 inches from ground to withers. The weight is to be under 7 pounds, with a weight from 4 to 6 pounds preferred. The AKC standard also states that overall quality is to be favored over size. Females may be as much as 2 pounds lighter than males. European Maltese can be heavier than 7 pounds, sometimes weighing as much as 9 pounds. That may not sound like much variation, but on a 7-pound dog, that's an additional 30%!

DESCRIPTION OF THE MALTESE

Overview

- The Maltese's most distinct physical feature is his long silky white coat, reaching to the ground, with a beautifully plumed, gracefully carried tail.
- The Maltese is a small and well-balanced dog, with free-flowing movement.
- The Maltese's head and expression are important features. All features of the head, including the dark eyes and black pigmentation, contribute to the charming, sweet expression.
- The Maltese should not be more than 10 inches tall. Weight varies in different countries, but even the heaviest Maltese is only 9 pounds.

Are You a Maltese Person?

As a Maltese person, you will probably be as sweet-natured as your dog, and you will need a good brain to keep up with his intelligence! Your Maltese will adore affection, so you will be able to bestow on him as much as your generous heart will allow. If you are full of fun yourself, you will have a lot in common with your Maltese, who, with his impish nature, is a vigorous little companion with a great sense of humor. He is a dog that has that

The breed's small size and portability are great benefits, as most Maltese owners like to have their dogs with them whenever they can.

certain "something" about him and often wears a rather self-satisfied expression, which you will find difficult to resist.

Your Maltese will be happy to join you for a daily walk, but if you plan to take your dog out for walks in dirty wet weather, you must be prepared to spend a long time grooming your dog upon your return home. Likely your Maltese won't enjoy a walk in the rain as much as he'll enjoy a walk in nice weather. Your Maltese will also be happy if you are willing to play games with him around the house or in the yard. Even toy breeds need exercise and plenty of things to stimulate their active brains.

You and your Maltese will develop a close rapport and you'll find that your angelic white pal is most affec-tionate with you. He is a very discriminating character and does not offer his licks and kisses to just anyone! If you have a lot of casual

The Maltese is as pretty as a picture, and just as beautiful in real life, too.

The Maltese is truly an irresistible breed. Who can hold back from showing her favorite Maltese how much she loves him?

CHAPTER 3

callers to your house, you should not expect your dog to show the same affection toward them. Because he is an individualist, the Maltese does not always take readily to strangers, so you will have to understand this and accept his likes and dislikes.

just as well, as he wears a white coat! Of course, if you enjoy hairdressing, the Maltese is certainly the breed for you, for you can spend endless hours bathing, blow drying and grooming. You and your Maltese will be able to enjoy each other's company during

While these Maltese should never be mistaken for toys, they are just as collectible! For those who have the time and space for multiple dogs, the Maltese is a popular choice.

If you are a clean person who likes to look well-put-together and who keeps a clean, tidy home, then you will appreciate the cleanliness of the Maltese, which is a fastidious little breed. This is

grooming sessions. This will be a time for heart-to-heart discussions, and you can be sure he won't give away your secrets! You should have gathered from what we've discussed thus far that your

Maltese will most certainly expect you to keep him inside your home, and not in a kennel situation!

The children in your life will love a Maltese, and he will very probably love them too, but they must be taught to treat him with respect. He is a tiny dog and could easily be hurt by fingers that tug too firmly on his coat. Some children are more boisterous than others, so keep your dog's well-being in mind when your children's friends (or friends' children) drop by.

Children can make a lot of noise. Generally, a Maltese can cope with this, probably better than you can yourself. However, your Maltese must always have the opportunity to retire from the chaos of daily life when he wishes to do so, and if you have a penchant for gentle classical music, he will probably appreciate a little of that, too. A simple wire crate in the house will serve as an ideal "getaway" for your Maltese

In addition to his crate, your Maltese will appreciate a soft, cozy bed in which he can cuddle up.

The Maltese may be small, but he's full of fun and energy to keep pace with the kids. Of course, with the breed's delicate size in mind, all playtime with children should be supervised and children taught the right way to handle the Maltese.

and is an excellent training device too. Because your Maltese will undoubtedly have to be left alone for short periods in his crate, such as when you go out to do the shopping, you will probably want to leave on a radio for him to listen to. A program that combines chat with light music is always a good option, so that he doesn't feel too alone.

As you are undoubtedly an animal lover, you may have other pets at home. You will therefore have to have the common sense to introduce to them to each other carefully, always keeping in mind that the newcomer is a Toy breed. The Maltese is a tough little character, but he is not so robust as a German Shepherd or Rottweiler! Successful introduction will depend more on the temperaments of your other pets, for Maltese are usually prepared to socialize with most animals. When your Maltese has chosen his closest friends, his relationship with them will be truly sincere, just as your own will be with him.

ARE YOU A MALTESE PERSON?

Overview

- A Maltese person is looking for a sweet, beautiful companion who has lots of affection to give to a dog.
- A Maltese person wants a toy dog with a charming, vibrant nature, equally ready to relax or to play.
- A Maltese person is ready to commit to the time and effort necessary to groom his dog, whether kept in full coat or clipped into a pet trim.
- A Maltese person always ensures his small dog's safety, making sure that others know how to handle the dog properly and supervising his interactions with other animals.

Selecting a Breeder

Because of the breed's sweet-tempered nature and breathtaking beauty, the Maltese is well-loved in most countries of the world, especially in the US, where the breed ranks high on our roster of favorite Toys.

Acquiring a well-bred Maltese will take some footwork on your part, as good breeders rarely have puppies available for sale right at the time that you want one. You should make your inquiries well in advance so that your name can be

Maltese generally have small litters, meaning that prospective owners will have to be patient in waiting for their perfect pup.

put on a waiting list. It's possible that you may find a good breeder with something immediately available but, especially if you want a puppy to take into the show ring, you should be prepared to wait. Unlike large breeds like Great Danes and Bloodhounds, whose litters can be 16 puppies or even more, Maltese litters can consist of a single puppy. A breeder's long-awaited litter could only satisfy the demand of one buyer.

It's hard to tell who's who in this newborn litter, so the breeder has given the pups blue and pink ribbons to differentiate between the boys and the girls.

Prospective puppy buyers should always keep foremost in their minds that there are many different kinds of breeder, some with the breed's interest at heart, others less dedicated. It is essential that you locate one who not only has dogs you admire but also breeding ethics with which you can agree. Sadly, in all breeds there are invariably some who are simply "in it for the money," and these you must give a wide berth. A poorly bred Maltese puppy is a sad

If you have aspirations to show your Maltese, you will need the breeder's advice as to which pup shows the most promise. Though no one can predict a dog's future quality for certain, the breeder's knowledge will be invaluable in guiding you in the right direction.

CHAPTER 4

sight indeed. If the puppy does not resemble one of the little angels in this book, you should keep looking. Even if you don't want a show-dog candidate, you have chosen the Maltese so that you can have a beautiful, charming, healthy home companion. Settle for nothing less.

There are many good breeders around and, if you look carefully, you will find just such a person. You must be as certain as you can be that the breeder fully understands his breed and has given careful consideration to the way the Maltese has been bred, taking into consideration each dog's pedigree and health. The Maltese Club of America is a trusted source of breeder referrals, as their members must follow a strict code of ethics in their breeding programs.

The breeder you select should be someone who breeds from home, in which case the puppies will have hopefully been brought up in the house and will be familiar with all the activities and noises that surround them. Even the larger breeding establishments whelp Maltese litters inside the home. In my personal opinion, this is infinitely better than the puppies' being raised in a kennel environment, especially for small breeds such as the Maltese.

However large or small the breeding establishment, it is important that the conditions in which the puppies are raised are suitable. All areas should be clean and the puppies should be well supervised in a suitable environment. All should all look in tiptop condition and temperaments should be sound, the puppies full of fun with plenty of confidence.

The breeder should be perfectly willing to introduce you to the dam, and it will be interesting for you to take careful note of her own

It goes without saying that the breeder's love of the Maltese should be undeniably evident.

temperament and how she interacts with her offspring. If the dam is not available for you to see, be forewarned that this might be a sign that the puppy was not born on the premises, but has been brought in from elsewhere to be sold. Do not purchase a puppy from a breeder who does not have the dam available. If the breeder tells

A big responsibility of breeders is to help the puppies through the weaning process and start them out on a quality diet that provides optimal nutrition at this crucial stage of development.

you that the dam of this litter is already "back on the show circuit," laugh and go home. No dam, after raising a litter of pups, is ready for the show ring, particularly a long-coated white breed of dog.

As for the stud dog, it is likely that he will not be on the premises, for he may well be owned by someone else. A careful breeder often will travel great distances to use a particular dog's stud services. Nonetheless, dedicated breeders will be able at least to show you a picture of the sire, along with his pedigree, and tell you all about him.

A well-chosen breeder will be able to give the new puppy owner lots of useful guidance, including advice about grooming and feeding. Some breeders give a small quantity of food to the new owners when the puppies leave for new homes. In any event, the breeder should always provide written details of exactly what type and quantity of food should be fed, and with what regularity. You will, of course, be able to change this as time goes on, but any changes must be gradual.

A breeder will also need to tell you what vaccinations the puppy has received, if any, and any relevant documentation should be passed over at the time of purchase. Details about the puppy's worming routine must also be made clear. Ask for the registration papers, pedigree, sales agreement and health guarantee. These are all reasonable requests from the buyer. Many breeders also provide temporary insurance coverage for the puppy. This is a good idea, and the new owner can subsequently decide whether or not to continue with this particular policy.

SELECTING A BREEDER

Overview

- Finding a Maltese breeder will not be difficult; it's finding a *reputable* breeder, an experienced and dedicated Maltese person, that will require more research, and this is the only source from which you should consider buying a puppy.
- Be prepared to wait for the right breeder and puppy.
- When visiting the breeder, look around the premises, meet the litter's parents—at least the dam—and observe the puppies. Be prepared with questions for the breeder.
- Likewise, the breeder will have many questions for you. This is a sign that he truly cares about the futures of his pups.
- Choose a breeder with whom you have a rapport, as he will be a valuable source of help throughout your Maltese's life with you.

Finding the Right Puppy

Although a puppy's bite will change as he grows, you should check your puppy's mouth and teeth for proper formation that will lead to the correct adult bite.

There is no disputing that a puppy Maltese is absolutely enchanting, his fuzzy white coat, not yet flowing to the ground, making you simply want to cuddle him and give him love and affection. However, you must bear in mind that this enchanting little puppy will grow into a fully coated adult whose coat will dangle on the floor. This will involve a good deal of care and attention, so please don't be deceived by the soft puppy coat.

A healthy puppy should strike you as being clean, without any sign of discharge from the eyes or nose. His rear end should be spotless, with no indication of loose bowels, which would be evident in the clear white coat of a Maltese. Although any puppy's nails can be sharp, they should not be too long, which would indicate that the breeder has not clipped them as necessary. Most breeders clip the puppies' nails so that they don't scratch their dam and siblings while nursing and playing.

With all of those sweet faces looking at you, it won't be easy to choose just one!

The coat should clearly be in excellent condition and there should be no knots or tangles in the coat nor any sign of parasites. Parasites such as fleas and lice cannot always be seen easily, but will be indicated by the puppy's scratching. You might also notice a rash. Scratching, though, does not always indicate a parasitic or skin condition, for it can also be associated with teething. In this case,

The contrast of dark eyes and white coat creates a dramatic appearance, giving even young puppies a "serious side" to their inquisitive puppy expressions.

CHAPTER 5

When you find your perfect puppy match, you'll know it!

the puppy will only scratch around his head area, and when the second set of teeth have come through so that the gums are no longer sore, this will stop.

Scratching might also be connected with an ear infection, so a quick look inside your new puppy's ears will ensure that there is no build-up of wax, and there should be no odor from the ears. Of course, a good breeder will have checked that the puppy is in good overall health before offering him for sale.

Find out about the most current screening require-ments for hereditary condi-tions in the breed. Breeders "screen" their stock (proven sires and dams) for the hereditary problems that may occur in the breed. Common in many pure-bred dogs are progressive retinal atrophy, hip and elbow dysplasia, patellar luxation and epilepsy, though not all

of these are documented in the Maltese. The Maltese Club of America can advise you of what problems its breeders are concerned about, and your chosen breeder should be able to discuss the screening of his stock with you. You must ask to see written proof of the test results, and remember to take note of the dates on which any tests were done.

Most puppies are outgoing and full of fun, so do not take pity on the overly shy one that hides away in a corner. Your puppy should clearly enjoy your company when you go along to visit, and this will make for a long-term bond between you. When you go to select your puppy, if possible take with you the members of your family with whom the puppy will spend time at home. It is essential that everyone in the family agrees with the important decision you are about to make, for a new puppy will inevitably change all of your lives.

You should already have done plenty of research about the breed before reaching the stage of having a new puppy enter your lives. Books about the Maltese, the Internet and breed-club pamphlets are helpful and handy sources to answer all of your questions about the breed. Breed clubs are indeed an important source of help and information. Some clubs publish a monthly or quarterly newsletters or even books of champions so that you can look back to see what your puppy's famous ancestors actually looked like. You can subscribe to one of the monthly canine magazines or try to find them for sale at

Belly up! Maltese puppies are brimming with personality and good humor.

your local pet shop. The dog-show weekly papers must be subscribed to or picked up at dog shows.

When using the Internet for information on the breed or breeders, you must be especially careful. I would urge you not to believe all you read! These days anyone can set up a website and can write what they like, even though they may not have sufficient knowledge of the breed to do so. Stick to trusted sources like the AKC, the American Maltese Association and their affiliate clubs and member breeders.

Finally, it is a good idea to become a member of at least one breed club. In doing so, you will meet other breed fanciers and learn about breed-specific events in which you may like to participate, thus providing further opportunities to learn about the Maltese.

FINDING THE RIGHT PUPPY

Overview

- All Maltese pups are adorable, with sparkling dark eyes and fuzzy white coats, but you must look beyond the cuteness to find one that's healthy and sound both physically and temperamentally.
- All pups in the litter should appear healthy, and the breeder should show you documentation of any genetic-disease testing and clearances on the parents and the litter.
- Spend some time with the litter, getting to know each pup's personality. The breeder's advice will also lead you to a good match.
- You have done much research on the Maltese before selecting your pup; be sure to continue your education once your pup comes home.

Welcoming the Maltese

It is almost certain that the wait for your Maltese puppy will seem like an eternity, but that time can be put to good use in preparing for the pup's arrival. Soon you will be able to collect your Maltese to bring home. For this momentous day, you will want to be certain that everything at home is as well prepared as it can possibly be. Because you have selected a long-coated breed, you will need to buy some grooming tools, especially if you plan to exhibit your puppy at shows.

You will need some basic grooming equipment for your new puppy. As you will spend much time grooming him during your life together, you should start accustoming him to the routine after he's had a few days to settle in.

It is expected that you will have had an opportunity to see and select your puppy before the date of collection. Should this be the case, you will have had plenty of chances to discuss with the breeder exactly what your puppy will need to make his life healthy, safe and also enjoyable.

The first time away from the company of his littermates, your pup is sure to experience loneliness. Give him lots of love and gently help him make the transition to his new family.

Depending on where you live, you will possibly have easy access to one of the large pet-supply outlets or a good privately owned pet shop. Many smaller shops are owned by experienced dog people, in which case they often have a wide range of items and will probably be able to give sensible guidance as to what you need to buy. Major dog shows also usually have a wide range of trade stands that cater to every need, and you are sure to have a superb selection of items from which to choose!

Keep in mind the Maltese's small size and small teeth when choosing appropriate safe chew toys.

Let's begin by discussing the grooming equipment that you will need for your Maltese puppy. Realize that you will have to add to this as your dog matures and the coat becomes more demanding. At this early stage, a soft bristle brush and high-quality comb will be your principal needs, and you will need tiny dental elastics with which to tie up your puppy's head hair. You will also need canine nail clippers.

You probably already have things like cotton balls and towels as household items.

Where your puppy is to sleep will be a major consideration, and you should start as you mean to go on. It is only natural that the newcomer will be restless for the first couple of nights or so, but if you immediately take pity on the little soul and let him join you in your bedroom, he will expect to remain there always! Hence it

A small-sized crate will suffice to accommodate your Maltese as a puppy and adult. Be sure to make the crate comfy with soft bedding, toys and other comforts to make it a home-within-a-home.

is essential that the bedding you choose should be eminently suitable so that your puppy can rest as comfortably as possible in the intended place.

The intended place, for expected for the first few weeks. In addition, you should give your puppy a small bed in which he can rest when he's spending time along with the family. Wicker beds may look pretty, but

You don't want fancy dog accessories to be ruined by potty accidents, so save the cute stuff until after house-training is accomplished. This Maltese cuddles up with a stuffed friend in his very own four-poster dog bed.

the sake of safety, house-breaking and general care, should be his crate. A small wire crate serves the needs of the Maltese perfectly. Inside the crate, you will want to provide a nice soft pillow or crate mat, something easily washable, since accidents in the puppy's crate must be they are dangerous because puppies chew them and sharp wicker pieces can all too easily injure eyes, be swallowed or become entangled in the coat. It is wiser to choose a durable bed that can be washed or wiped down. This can easily be lined with comfortable soft bedding that can be washed frequently, for it is important that all of your dog's bedding is kept clean and dry. You should also choose a bed that is either just slightly raised from the ground or otherwise positioned so that it will avoid drafts.

Although the Maltese is small, this is an active breed and can get into all kinds of mischief. Everyday household items may seem harmless enough, but a dainty cloth draped over the side of a little table full of fragile ornaments is just asking for trouble! Even more dangerous to a mischievous puppy are electric cables, so be sure they are concealed from his reach. Tiny teeth can bite though all too easily, causing what can be a fatal accident. Another word of warning concerns cleaning agents and gardening aids. Many of these contain substances that are poisonous, so please keep them out of the way of temptation. Antifreeze is especially dangerous. It tastes good to dogs, but just a small amount can kill a dog quickly.

When your puppy first arrives home, it is only natural that you will be excited and will want to show your new companion to your friends. However, your puppy is making a

A puppy uses his mouth to explore and can be suprisingly quick about picking things up off the ground. For his safety, the only things he should be chewing on are his food, treats and toys that you give him.

big move in his little life, so the first two or three days are best spent quietly at home with you and your immediate family. When your puppy has found his feet and taken stock of his new surroundings, you will be able to introduce him to lots of new people. If you have young children, or if they visit, always carefully supervise any time spent with your puppy. Youngsters are often attracted by the coat of a Maltese, and little fingers can all too easily tug at the coat and hurt the puppy, even with the best of intentions.

Children must be taught that a toy dog is not a toy.

If your family has other pets, introductions should be made slowly and under close supervision. Most Maltese get along well with other animals, but you should always exercise caution until you are certain that all concerned are going to be the best of friends. Don't forget that the Maltese is tiny, and larger dogs may be too rough for the Maltese to handle, even just in friendly play.

WELCOMING THE MALTESE

Overview

- Before your puppy comes home, be prepared for his arrival. Have all of the necessary accessories on hand.
- Choose a suitable sleeping area for your puppy and plan on having him sleep there from the very first night.
- All dogs are curious and more than capable of getting into trouble, so protect both your home and your puppy by removing all potential dangers from the home, indoors and out.
- Don't overwhelm puppy during his first few days. Make all introductions low-key and allow him time to get acclimated.

Your Puppy's Education

Any young puppy needs time to adapt to his new surroundings, and the Maltese is no exception. After all, your tiny puppy will be entering a strange new world, where nothing is familiar to him. Sights, sounds and smells will all be different, so when the youngster first arrives home, begin by getting him used to the members of your family, allowing him time to take stock of his new environment. Be sure to instill confidence into your puppy to help with his early socialization. Soon enough, you will be

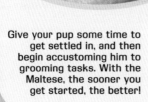

Give your pup some time to get settled in, and then begin accustoming him to grooming tasks. With the Maltese, the sooner you get started, the better!

able to introduce him to people outside the immediate family. It is important that your Maltese puppy is not bombarded with too many new people and situations all at the same time.

Depending on the age of your puppy, and whether his course of vaccinations is complete, you may or may not be able to take him out in public places immediately. Whichever the case, I would still advise you to allow him to settle down at home for the first few days before venturing further. There will be lots you can do with your Maltese puppy at home. You will surely have a lot of fun, but please allow your puppy to get sufficient rest, too.

If restricted to your home territory for a little while, you can play games with him with suitably safe soft toys, but do not allow him to tug on anything too strongly, as you do not want to cause chaos to the tooth

Your Maltese won't take up too much room on your favorite chair, but will your dog be allowed on the furniture or not? Decide on this and other house rules when your Maltese is a pup, and enforce all of them consistently.

The first few days with your pup will likely be spent close to home, giving him affection and reassurance, and perhaps even a guided tour of the yard.

formation. Check regularly that sharp or unsafe parts, such as squeaks, do not become detached from or torn out of the toy. These can cause injury, and your puppy's teeth will be very sharp and capable of easily damaging soft toys.

Whether or not you plan to show your Maltese, it is always good to do a little early training, getting him to stand calmly on a table and to lie on his side to be gently groomed. Both will be helpful on numerous occasions, including visits to the vet, when it is much easier to deal with a well-behaved dog, and you will be so proud of your clever companion!

Accustom your puppy to being on a lead, which is always a strange experience for a tiny youngster. Begin by putting just a simple collar on him, not too tightly, but not so loose that it can be caught on things, causing panic and possible injury. Just put it on for a few minutes at a time, lengthening each period slightly until your puppy feels comfortable in his first item of clothing. Don't expect miracles; this may take a few days.

Then, when he is comfortable in his collar, attach a small lightweight lead. The one you select must have a secure catch, yet be simple to attach and release as necessary. Until now, your puppy has simply gone where he has pleased and will find it very strange to be attached to someone who is restricting his movements. For this reason, when training my own puppies, I like to allow them to "take" me for the first few sessions, then I begin to guide them gently. Soon enough, training can start in earnest, with the puppy coming with me as I lead the way.

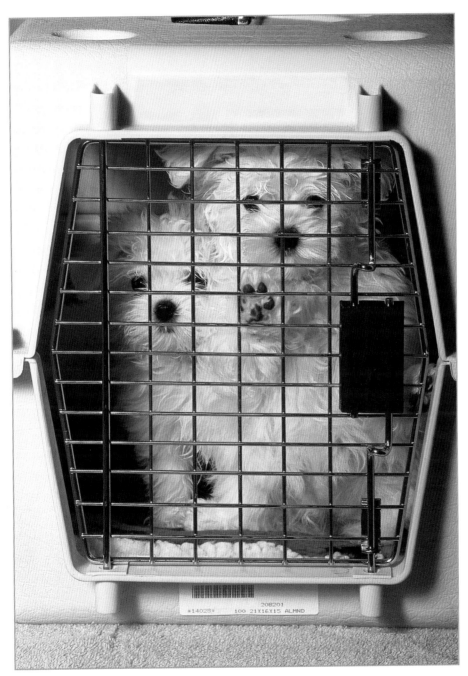

If the breeder has introduced the litter to crates, even just briefly, he has done you a big favor by starting off on the right "paw" with crate-training.

A lightweight yet sturdily made nylon collar and lead, like the ones shown, will suffice for a Maltese puppy and adult. Be sure to check and adjust the collar regularly with the puppy's growth.

It is usual to begin training the puppy to walk on your left-hand side. When this has been accomplished to your satisfaction, you can try moving him on your right, but there is absolutely no hurry. If you plan to show your Maltese, you will generally move your dog on your left, but there are occasions when it is necessary also to move him on your right so as not to obstruct the judge's view.

As your puppy gets older, you can teach him to sit, always using a simple one-word command. Tell him to "sit" while holding a food treat above his head, and possibly placing the palm of your hand behind his rump. You should not have to exert any pressure on his rear to show him what you expect, but this could serve as a final option. This lesson will take a little time, but you will soon succeed, always giving plenty of praise when appro-priate. Never shout or get angry when your dog does not achieve your aim, for this will do more harm than good. As a sidebar, if yours is destined to be a show dog, you may decide not to teach the sit command, as in the show ring he will be expected to stand.

When your Maltese puppy is properly vaccinated and can venture into public places, begin by taking him somewhere quiet without too many distractions. Soon you will find his confidence increasing and you can then introduce him to new places with exciting sights, sounds and smells. He must always be on a safe lead that cannot be slipped (quite different from the type used in the show ring). When you have total confidence in one another, you will probably be able to let him off lead. Always keep him in sight and be sure the place you have chosen for free exercise is utterly safe and securely enclosed.

Certainly if you have a show dog, and most likely if you have a pet, you will need to train your puppy to stay in a crate when required. At most dog shows, Toy breeds are housed in crates for at least part of the time while not being actually exhibited in the ring. Crates are useful

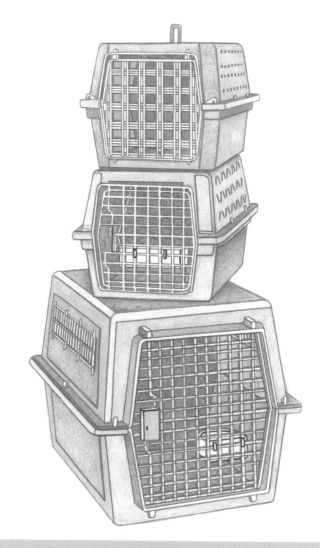

It's no trouble to transport the tiny Maltese. A sturdy fiberglass crate with a handle on top makes a safe and easy-to-carry way for the Maltese to travel.

for traveling and, if used in the home, most dogs seem to look upon them as safe places to go and don't mind staying in their crates for short periods. You also will appreciate the crate's usefulness for house-training.

When you commence crate training, remain within sight of your dog and give him a toy, something safe and constructive to occupy his mind in the crate. To begin, leave him in the crate for very short spells of just a minute or two, then gradually build up the time span. However, never confine a dog to a crate for long periods, for that would be unkind.

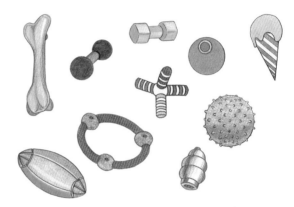

Visit your pet shop for fun, safe, interactive toys.

YOUR PUPPY'S EDUCATION

Overview

- Once your pup is used to his new family and surroundings, and properly vaccinated, begin socialization to the outside world.
- Early lessons can include introduction to the grooming table and basic grooming procedures.
- Let your puppy become comfortable with his collar and lead and then proceed to taking short on-lead walks.
- Introduce your pup informally to the basic commands before real training begins.
- Let your pup explore his crate and begin to instill in him a positive association with it.

House-training Your Maltese

The Maltese is a very clean little breed that appreciates his surroundings being as spotless as he likes to be himself, so if you are consistent in your methods of training, your Maltese should learn quickly. To house-train with success, you will need to be firm, but never harsh, and you must certainly never be rough with your Maltese.

When your puppy first arrives in

For newborn puppies, their whelping box functions as living room, bedroom, kitchen and, of course, bathroom. The box is lined with absorbent materials, and a good breeder will be diligent about its cleanliness.

your home, he may or may not already be house-trained, albeit to a limited extent. However, you must always realize that your home is completely different from the breeder's, so he will have to re-learn the house rules. Doors will not be located in the same places, your family may go to bed and rise at different times, and it will undoubtedly take him a little time to learn and to adapt.

The Maltese is a clean dog that will want to adopt clean habits. You must do your part, too, by always keeping the yard free of droppings so your dog has a clean place to play.

The speed of your house-training success will depend to a certain extent on your living environment and the season of the year. Most puppies are perfectly happy to go out into the yard in dry weather, but when rain is teeming down, most feel rather differently and will need considerable encouragement!

Paper training is always useful in the very early stages of training. Paper should be placed by the door so that the dog learns to associate the

If you don't have a yard in which your Maltese can do his business, you must take him out on his lead several times a day, sticking to a schedule and of course bringing your "poop scoop."

paper with the exit to the wide world outside. When he uses the paper, he should be praised. Obviously, it is ideal if the puppy can be let out as soon as he shows any sign of wanting to do his business, but again this may depend on whether your home has immediate access to a back yard.

Here's why and how that shiny wire crate solves all of your housebreaking concerns for your Maltese. Crate training is based on a simple canine precept: dogs don't mess where they sleep. Your Maltese is a classy gentleman or lady and, of course, relishes clean bedding. This is true not only of your elegant toy dog but also others—purebreds and mutts alike. All dogs keep their sleeping areas clean. The crate serves as the dog's sleeping area and, therefore, the dog will make every effort to keep his crate clean.

Put your Maltese in his

A wire crate is good to use as your Maltese's special place in the home. It offers the dog unobstructed ventilation and a clear view of what's going on around him while safely confined.

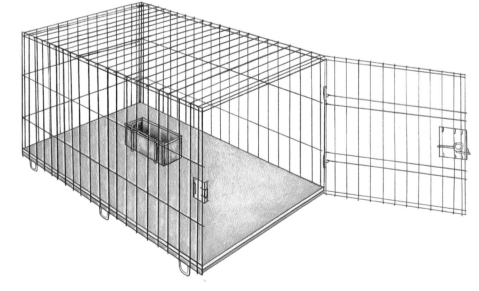

crate at night. He will learn to sleep in his crate once he discovers that his whining and carrying-on leads to

trainers recommend feeding the dog in the crate for the first few meals so that he associates it with happy

Teaching your puppy proper toileting habits is the key to having a clean dog with whom it is a pleasure to share your home.

nothing. (Ignore your whining baby. He does not have a wet diaper! He'll fall asleep.) During the day, your Maltese will use his crate for naps and playtime. Some

times. Give him a small biscuit when he goes in his crate. One! Don't think you're doing him any favors by giving him a dozen biscuits, because he'll have to relieve himself and, thus, you're defeating your purposes of using the crate.

Every time you release the puppy from his crate, bring him outside to his potty area (or to the newspaper, if you live in a high-rise apartment or don't have a convenient outdoor area). Praise him for every drop! He'll understand and want to please you.

Remember that puppies need to go out much more frequently than adult animals, certainly immediately after waking and following a meal. In fact, to take your pup outside every hour while he is awake is not a bad idea at all. Always keep both your eyes and ears open, for a youngster will not be able to wait those extra two or three minutes until it is convenient for you to let him out. If you delay, accidents will certainly happen, so be warned! It surely sounds like half of your day will be spent leading your Maltese outside for his potty trips. Welcome to dog ownership—it's not all glamour owning a Maltese.

As your puppy matures, asking to be let out when necessary will become second nature, and it is rare to encounter a Maltese that is unclean in the house. A stud dog, however, can be different, for he may well want to mark his territory, and your table and chair legs may be just the places he decides to choose! Males, in general, are a little slower to housebreak than females. Most attribute this to the male's fixation with his private parts and the need to leave his mark on every vertical object in the world.

Simple commands are very helpful, "Potty time" being an old favorite, and it seems to work. You can choose any command you like, but don't be too clever, cute or crude as one day you may be embarrassed when you have to announce give verbal reprimand, but this will only work if your Maltese is caught in the act. If you try to reprimand him

With puppies, what goes in must come out—quickly! The breeder keeps the litter on some type of absorbent material at all times.

"Poopie!" to your house full of guests.

Never, ever forget to give praise when the deed is done in the desired place. However, if an accident happens, you should indeed after the event, he will simply not know what he has done wrong, and this will only serve to confuse.

It is essential that any mess be cleaned up immediately. If your dog has done

CHAPTER 8

This Maltese has quite the setup! The door leads to a covered area, lined with paper, in which he can relieve himself in bad weather.

You pick the area for your Maltese's relief site, so choose wisely. An out-of-the way spot, rather than flowerbeds or high-traffic areas, is obviously the best choice.

his toilet in the wrong place, it must be cleaned thoroughly so as to disguise the smell or he will want to use that particular place again. Pet shops sell excellent deodorizers designed to clean stains and remove pet odors from human and canine noses. Likewise, you can use conventional cleaning products, but never anything that is pine-based, as it can be harmful to dogs.

When your puppy is old enough to be exercised in public places, always carry with you a "pooper scoop" or small plastic bag so that any droppings can be removed. Most cites and towns have laws about this, so be a clean, law-abiding dog owner. You don't want the police blotter to say you were thrown in the slammer for not scooping!

HOUSE-TRAINING YOUR MALTESE

Overview

- The key to clean living with your dog is teaching your Maltese proper toileting habits.
- Paper training can help you get started, but crate training is the most reliable way to house-train a dog.
- Take your puppy out very frequently, using a consistent "potty" command and praising him when he goes in the right spot.
- Never reprimand your pup for accidents in the home unless you catch him in the act.
- Pet shops sell excellent products to clean stains and remove pet odors.
- Don't forget to be a good dog-owning citizen and always clean up after your Maltese.

CHAPTER 9

Teaching Basic Commands

The intelligence of the Maltese makes this a breed that is highly capable of learning. To have training success, your Maltese will expect to be given a reason why he should do something. The Maltese will certainly not take kindly to harsh training, nor to harsh words, so be consistent and gentle in your approach, always giving plenty of praise at the close of an exercise. Common sense tells you that dogs, like children, respond better to praise and treats than they do to reprimands and punishment.

Whether you have a home

The bright little Maltese makes an eager and alert student, amenable to training and able to learn quickly.

companion or a show dog, your Maltese should learn the basic obedience commands. Some show handlers, however, do not train their dogs to sit on command, since this is a position that is unnecessary in the show ring. In all training, it is essential to get your dog's full attention, which many owners do with the aid of treats so that the dog learns to associate treats with praise.

The sit is one of the first exercises you will teach; the sit/stay, shown here, is a little more advanced.

The following training method involves using food treats, although you will wean your dog off these training aids in time so that your rewards are mostly praise and petting. Always use very simple commands, just one or two short words, and keep training sessions short so they do not become boring for your dog.

In order to have success in training, there must be good communication between dog and owner. The basis of this is the dog's attention, which must be focused on his owner like this attentive pupil.

SIT COMMAND

For most dogs, here's a great place to start. Sitting is a natural posture for most dogs and is therefore an easy exercise to accomplish. With the lead in your left hand, hold a small treat in your right, letting your dog smell or lick the treat but not take it. Move it away as you say "Sit," your hand rising slowly over the dog's head so that he looks upward. In doing so, he will bend his knees and sit. When this has been accomplished, give the reward and lavish praise.

If your Maltese starts to back up when you raise the food treat over his head, his way of keeping his eye on the liver, you're going to have to make this a two-handed operation. Place your palm behind your Maltese's rear end, and when he backs up to see the food treat, he'll feel your hand and naturally go into a sit position. Practice the exercise this way a few times and soon the dog will understand that he is

expected to sit. Always praise him after every successful exercise.

HEEL COMMAND
A dog trained to walk to heel will walk alongside his handler without pulling. Again the lead should be held in your left hand while the dog assumes the sit position next to your left leg. Hold the end of the lead in your right hand, but also control it lower down with your left.

Step forward with your left foot, saying the word "Heel." To begin, take just three steps, then command him to sit again. Repeat this procedure until he carries out the task without pulling. Then you can increase the number of strides to five, seven and so on. Give verbal praise at the close of each section of the exercise and, at the end of the training session, let him enjoy himself with a free run.

Never use an on-lead walk to be your Maltese's wild running time. He will associate the lead with this and you will never convince him that it's necessary to walk calmly by your side. It's a lot more fun to run in circles at full speed! The lead, from the first day, must indicate to the dog that it's a structured exercise.

DOWN COMMAND

When your dog is proficient in sitting, you can introduce the word "Down." It is first essential to understand that a dog will consider the down position as a submissive one, so gentle training is important.

With your Maltese sitting by your left leg, as for the sit, hold the lead in your left

Gently guide your Maltese into the sit position for the first few tries, and he will soon learn what is expected of him.

hand and a treat in your right. Place your left hand on top of the dog's shoulders (without pushing) and hold the treat under his nose, saying "Down" softly but convincingly. Gradually move the treat along the floor, in front of the dog, all the while talking gently. He will follow this, lowering himself down. When his elbows touch the floor, you can release the treat and give praise, but try to get him to remain there for a few seconds before getting up. Gradually the time of the down exercise can be increased.

Some toy dogs don't respond to the down exercise too readily—partially because they're already pretty close to the floor in the first place. You can try to teach the down command with your Maltese on your lap, facing forward. You will use the food treat at the dog's nose and lower it below the level of your lap. The dog will squat down and assume the desired position. After you've practiced the command a few times this way, you can place the puppy on the chair or couch next to you and try it there. Always praise the puppy for assuming the position. Once your Maltese recognizes the command, you can begin to work on the floor again.

STAND COMMAND
There will be many occasions when you need your dog to stand still. Your veterinarian will appreciate your efforts if you have trained your Maltese to stand still for his examination. Likewise, if yours is a show dog, your Maltese will be highly regarded in the show ring if he can stand perfectly statuesque while the judge is reviewing him. In everyday life, you may want your Maltese to stand by your side when you come

to an intersection, especially on a rainy day when the usual sit position (part of the heel lesson) isn't particularly smart. During grooming sessions, the stand and down positions will be useful.

Begin with the puppy sitting on your left side. Hold the lead in your left hand and a food treat in your right hand, and place the food treat at the dog's nose so that he can see it. As you move your hand slowly forward, the dog will stand to be closer to the treat. Say "Stand." Give him the treat and praise him. You can use the lead to propel the dog forward, though this may not be necessary.

STAY COMMAND

Stay can be taught with your dog in either a sit, stand or down position, as usual with the lead in your left hand and the treat in your right. Allow him to lick the treat as you say "Stay," while standing directly in front of the dog, having moved from

Even though your Maltese is low to the ground, he may, as with many dogs, not like the down position. Approach it with encouragement, and you'll be on to the down/stay in no time.

your position at his right side. Silently count to about five, then move back to your original position alongside him. Allow your dog to have the treat while giving him lavish praise.

Keep practicing the stay command just as described for a few days, then gradually increase the distance between you, using

Keep your Maltese on lead when beginning the stay exercise. Once you progress to farther distances and take him off his lead, be sure to practice in a securely enclosed area.

your hand with the palm facing to the dog as an indication that he must stay. Soon you should be able to do this exercise without a lead and your Maltese will stay for increasingly longer periods of time. Always give lavish praise upon completion of the exercise.

COME COMMAND
Your Maltese will love to come back to you when called. The idea is to invite him to return, offering a treat and giving lots of praise when he does so. It is important to teach the come command, for this should bring your dog running back to you if ever he is in danger of moving out of sight.

As with all commands, keep the come exercise light and gay. This is positive training we're using here. No dog, especially one as bright as the Maltese, will come to you if you sound as if you're not happy. Dogs respond to joy—clapping, high-pitched sounds, your elation to see them. Use this when teaching the come exercise. Your Maltese should always think that coming to you will lead to good things, never punishment or scolding.

The Maltese is the height of canine fashion— posing on the runway with the breed's sparkling star quality.

KEEP PRACTICING

Ongoing practice is actually a lifetime dog rule. Incorporate these commands into your daily routine, and your Maltese will remain a gentleman or lady of whom you can be proud!

TEACHING BASIC COMMANDS

Overview

- All dogs need an education in basic commands in order to be well mannered and reliable.
- Your bright Maltese is an excellent pupil and will learn new exercises quickly.
- Positive reinforcement is the best way to train any dog, using rewards of praise, petting and treats.
- The basic commands include sit, heel, down, stand, stay and come.
- Keep practicing with your Maltese and incorporate the basic commands into your daily routine.

Home Care for Your Maltese

Your Maltese will be very precious to you, so you are sure to want to keep him in the very best of health throughout his life, which you hope will be a long one. This means that routine care on a daily basis will be very important, for it will help you to see problems arising so that you can take your pet to the vet without delay for further investigation.

Home dental care is of utmost importance for your Maltese to maintain a strong, healthy bite, as Toy breeds tend to have trouble with their teeth.

DENTAL CARE

Owners must keep their smiling toy dogs' teeth white and shiny! Keeping teeth in good condition is your responsibility. You owe this to your dog, for dental problems do not just stop inside the mouth. When gums are infected, all sorts of heath problems can subsequently arise, spreading through the system and possibly leading even to consequent death.

Safe toys provide dental benefits as they minimize tartar as the dog chews—but don't offer a plaything that's too big for your Maltese!

You may clean the teeth of your Maltese extremely gently and carefully, using a very small tooth-brush and special canine toothpaste. Take particular care if any of the teeth are beginning to loosen. Your dog may not like this procedure much at first, but should easily get used to it if you clean regularly. Experienced breeders sometimes use a special dental scraper, but damage can be done with this, especially on a toy breed, so I do not recommended it for use by the average pet owner.

Special toothbrushes are designed for dogs of all sizes, made to fit the contours of the canine mouth.

When cleaning the teeth, always check the gums for signs of inflam-mation. If you notice that the gums look red or swollen, a visit to your vet would be worthwhile. Unfortunately, toy dogs are notorious for having inferior dental health, often marred by misaligned teeth, overshot bites and missing teeth. Some breed standards even allow for faults in complete dentition. Give your Maltese a biting chance—clean his teeth regularly.

FIRST AID

It pays to be prepared, as the old Boy Scout mantra preaches. When your dog's life is on the line, you will be glad that you have thought clearly ahead

Every dog can be a couch potato from time to time, but if your Maltese is acting lethargic or otherwise "off," this is a signal to call the vet.

(and flagged this page in the book!). Here are some accidents that can occur with your dog and commonsense ways to handle them while awaiting veterinary advice.

Insect stings are quite frequent and, if it still there, the "stinger" should be removed with tweezers. Ice can be applied to reduce the swelling and accurate dosage (ask your vet) of antihistamine treatment given. If a sting is inside the mouth, consult your vet at once.

Accidental poisoning is also a worry, as dogs can investigate all sorts of things, not all of which are safe. If you suspect poisoning, try to ascertain the cause, because treatment may vary according to the type of poison taken. Vomiting and sudden bleeding from an exit point, such as the gums, can be indications of poisoning. Urgent veterinary attention is essential.

Small abrasions should be cleaned thoroughly and have

antiseptic applied, but in the case of serious bleeding, initially apply pressure above the area. For minor burns, apply cool water.

In the case of shock, such as following a car accident, keep the dog warm while

die quickly from heat stroke, so urgent veterinary attention is of paramount importance. Conversely, in the case of hypothermia, keep the dog warm with hot-water bottles, and give a warm bath if possible.

Part of caring for your Maltese's ears is keeping them free of excess hair by gently plucking it out. This is painless for the dog if done correctly.

veterinary aid is sought without delay.

For heat stroke, cold water must be applied immediately, especially over the shoulders. In severe cases, if possible, the dog should be submerged in water up to his neck. Dogs can

RECOGNIZING HEALTH SIGNS

If you love your Maltese and you spend plenty of time together, you will know when something is amiss. He may lose his appetite or seem dull and listless, possibly carrying his tail down. His eyes, usually bright and alive, may seem to have lost their sparkle, and his coat may look dull and lackluster. His bathroom habits may also be an indication of ill health. Loose movements usually clear up within 24 hours, but if they go on for longer than this, especially if you see blood, you will need to visit your vet. Also keep a lookout for increased thirst and an increase in frequency of urination, which could indicate a problem.

CHECKING FOR PARASITES

It is essential to keep your dog's coat in first-rate order, or parasites may take hold, causing coat and skin condition to deteriorate. It is often not easy to see parasites, and if you catch sight of even one flea you can be sure there will be more lurking somewhere. There are now several good preventative aids available for external parasites, and your vet will be able to advise you about them, for the most effective remedies often are not available over the counter.

Also be on a continual lookout for ear mites. They cannot be seen, but a brown discharge with some odor coming from the ear is a clear indication that they are present. A suitable ear treatment will be available from your vet.

A dog can also carry internal parasites in the form of worms. Ascarids are the most common, and tapeworms, although less frequent, can be even more debilitating. Discuss preventatives with your veterinarian.

Heartworms are transmitted by mosquitoes and pose a serious problem for dogs.

Owners of light-colored dogs must deal with cleaning tear stains from around the eyes. Specially formulated cleansing products are made for this purpose.

Depending on where you live, your vet can advise you in the best way of protecting your dog. Of course, the Maltese is an indoor dog primarily and his exposure to wooded areas (and mosquitoes) is fairly limited. There aren't too many Maltese earning their daily biscuit by hunting quail in the woods! If you live in an area where mosquitoes are not present, you are probably fine not to give your dog heartworm preventative or to opt to give the monthly dose every other month. Some heartworm preventatives also protect against some of the other intestinal parasites.

Routine worming is essential throughout a dog's life and, again, veterinary recommendation as to a suitable regimen is certainly advised.

Home care for your dog means keeping the dog safe in the home. Baby gates or similar enclosures are helpful for keeping dogs confined to dog-proof areas.

HOME CARE FOR YOUR MALTESE

Overview

- Your dog's overall health, longevity and quality of life depend largely on the care he gets from you at home.
- Dental care is of utmost importance with a toy breed, as they are prone to teeth problems that can progress to have serious consequences.
- Educate yourself in basic canine first-aid techniques and have a well-stocked first-aid kit.
- Know your dog well so you will recognize any changes that could be symptoms of a health problem.

Feeding Your Maltese

Generally speaking, Maltese are fairly good eaters, but some can be a little finicky about their food. Some are undoubtedly allowed to eat the finest foods from expensive porcelain plates or crystal bowls, and they will have absolutely no objection to this! This is not necessary, however, so don't pander too much to your pet's whims.

When selecting the best diet, you should always consider that the Maltese is a toy breed. The food you offer should always be cut into small

Take your breeder's advice regarding how best to continue feeding your puppy, including schedule, amounts and how to change the diet appropriately as the puppy matures.

pieces if it is fresh food, and the commercial-brand dry variety should be what is usually known as "small bite." Most manufacturers offer this type for toy and other small dogs.

Today there is an enormous range of specially prepared foods available for dogs, many of them scientifically balanced and suitable for the different age ranges. You will begin your Maltese puppy on a puppy food. During his life, you may switch him to junior, adult and senior foods, as necessary. It is really a matter of personal preference as to which particular brand of food you decide to use, though initially this will be influenced by what has been fed to your new puppy by his breeder. Changes can, of course, be made, but never change suddenly from one food to another or your Maltese is likely to get an upset tummy. Introduce a new brand of food gradually over a few days, until the old brand is phased

The breeder starts the litter out on solid food as part of the weaning process. The diet at this time often consists of meat mixed with a quality puppy food.

Providing for a hungry litter is no small task for the dam. The breeder must be as attentive to her care as he is to that of the pups.

out. There is usually no harm at all in changing the flavor of food while keeping with the same brand. This can add some variety to the diet, or you might prefer to add a little flavored stock to tempt the palate.

Watch the crowd gather when there's a tasty reward at stake!

Make sure that you thoroughly read the feeding instructions for whichever commercially prepared dry food you select. Some of these need to be moistened, especially those for young-

sters. Dry food should be stored carefully, bearing in mind that its vitamin value declines if not used fairly quickly, usually within about three months. It is essential that a plentiful supply of fresh water is available for your dog when feeding dried foods in particular, though dogs should, of course, have access to water at all times.

Because of the enormous range of products available, you may find it difficult to decide which to choose without advice from another Maltese enthusiast. However, keep in mind that in adulthood an active dog will require a higher protein content than one that lives a sedentary life.

Whether it's the overwhelming selection of commercial foods available or simply the decision to not feed their dogs "from a bag," some owners prefer to feed fresh foods to their Maltese. In such cases, owners must

The best possible nutrition for the pups' first few weeks in life comes from their mother's milk, as it nourishes them and provides them with resistance to disease.

be absolutely certain that they are feeding a well-balanced diet and that no dangerous things like cooked bones are included in the meals. Vitamin and other supplements may be required with home-prepared diets. A fresh-food diet should only be attempted by an owner who is educated in how to prepare the diet safely and for complete nutrition.

Proper nutrition will be evident in a healthy lustrous coat and overall good condition.

Many owners are tempted to feed tidbits between meals, but this is not a good idea. Weight can pile on almost imperceptibly, especially on a tiny dog like a Maltese. A very suitable alternative is to give the occasional piece of carrot. Most dogs love them! Carrots don't put on any weight and are a useful aid to keeping the teeth clean. Table scraps should be avoided, keeping in mind that certain "people foods" like chocolate, onions, grapes, raisins and some nuts are toxic to dogs.

How many

A good-quality age-appropriate diet, along with plenty of fresh water, is essential at all stages of your Maltese's life.

times a day you feed your adult Maltese will probably be a matter of preference. Many people feed a small amount morning and evening; others prefer to give just one meal, perhaps with a light snack at the other end of the day. Obviously, puppies need to be fed more frequently, but your dog's breeder will hopefully have given you good advice in this regard, and the transition from the puppy schedule to one or two meals a day will be made gradually.

As a dog gets older, his metabolism changes, so feeding requirements may again change. An older dog is usually better able to digest smaller portions, so his daily food portion can be divided into smaller, more frequent meals. By then you will know your pet well and should be able to adjust his feeding accordingly, but if you have any queries about feeding your senior Maltese, your veterinarian should be able to guide you in the right direction.

FEEDING YOUR MALTESE

Overview

- Choose a quality food appropriate to your Maltese's age, size and activity level. Dog-food manufacturers make foods specifically formulated for all stages of a dog's life.
- Maltese do best with "small bite" food for their tiny teeth and mouths.
- Don't overdo it with treats, be careful about table scraps and know which "people foods" are toxic to dogs.
- Water is an essential component of a dog's diet, too.
- Your breeder and vet can advise you about dietary changes throughout your dog's life, including amounts, schedules and types of food.

Grooming Your Maltese

The breed you have so carefully chosen has a long white flowing coat that falls to the ground, so you will have your work cut out to keep it in top condition.

Grooming will now play an increasingly large part in your life!

Some pet owners like to keep their Maltese in short coat, possibly with the help of a professional groomer. A pet trim will necessitate visits every six to eight weeks and your careful attention in between. You will still need to spend

A few minutes a day, using a soft brush and gentle strokes, will help your puppy create a positive association with his grooming sessions.

time grooming your Maltese. Although the pet trim is far less time-consuming, it will still be very important to groom.

ROUTINE COAT CARE

Whether you keep the coat of your Maltese long or short, regular grooming must be introduced from a very early age. Even within the first three or four days of owning your new puppy, a few minutes daily should be set aside, teaching the little one to stand on a solid table and accept grooming very gently with a soft brush. When he is used to standing, teach him to lie over on his side, for you will find it much easier to groom a fully-coated Maltese and reach all the awkward places with the dog in this position.

The long facial furnishings must be combed out gently, taking special care in this sensitive area.

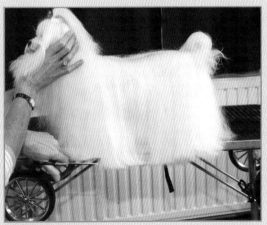

The Maltese's coat should be trimmed to floor length. The edge of the grooming table is a helpful guide to trimming the hair to the proper length in a straight line.

Grooming sessions will lengthen in time with maturity of coat. You must always be certain that your grooming equipment is kept clean so that it does not cause the hair to snag. Take care, too, that you do not mistakenly use a comb with missing teeth, for this can damage the coat and can even catch the skin.

Show dogs are usually bathed before each exhibition, but a pet Maltese can be bathed less frequently. In any event, the coat should always be groomed through before bathing. Before putting your Maltese in the bath, test the water temperature on the back of your hand. After wetting the coat, stroke in the shampoo rather than rub, for the latter will create knots. Select a shampoo designed especially for a white coat. The shampoo must always be rinsed out thoroughly before applying a conditioner, which should also be completely rinsed away.

Always use canine shampoo and conditioner rather than those designed for human hair, although you might like to use a baby shampoo on the head to avoid irritation to the eyes. When towel-drying the coat before using the blow dryer, pat rather than rub, again to avoid making knots.

When drying, it is important to groom the coat through as you do so. If you just leave the coat to dry naturally, or blow dry without brushing, you will have a very unkempt-looking Maltese on your hands! To get the best effect, you should work systematically, one area at a time, keeping the rest of the coat in a damp towel until it is dried with the blow dryer. Many dogs do not like hot air blowing into their faces, so please take this into consideration when drying.

When grooming without bathing, it is important to use a conditioning spray, or at least a water spray. If you groom a completely dry coat, the ends will break. Anti-tangle or conditioning spray should be applied generously to any tangles. Leave it in for a few minutes, then tease out the tangle carefully from the inside outward, using your

comfort, but not too short or it can cause aggravation.

As your Maltese matures, the head furnishings will increase in length. Your puppy must be trained to keep still while the head hair is

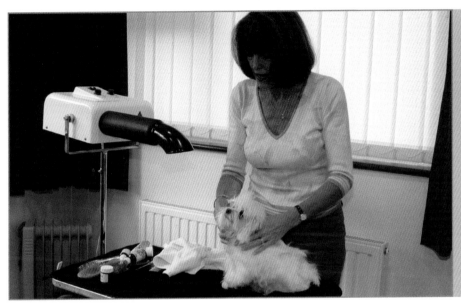

The dryer should be set on low heat, at a comfortable distance from the dog. Be sure to brush through the coat as you dry to keep it tangle-free.

fingers or a wide-toothed comb.

You will need to carefully trim below the foot pads so that hairballs do not form below the feet. Also, if yours is a male, the long hair that grows down from the penis should be trimmed slightly for

groomed and the topknot put into place. There are varying ways of presenting the head furnishings, either in a single topknot or double. After the hair has been brushed up from the eyes, the tip of the comb is used to draw a line from the outer corner of each eye, up to just before the edge of the ears. A line is drawn across the skull and the hair is then attached using a small dental elastic, never too tightly.

A double topknot is made by making a central parting

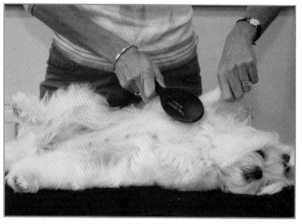

It is helpful to train your Maltese to lie on his side for part of the grooming process, as this position provides you access to some of the hard-to-reach areas, like the "armpits," which can be especially prone to matting.

between the eyes, forming a topknot on each side of the part. Maltese look very sweet when one or two little bows have been attached to give that final finishing touch. Always take care never to pull out an elastic when it is being changed. Instead, it should always be cut out, taking extreme care not to cut into the coat!

Another important final touch is the part that runs from the behind the topknot all the way to the tail. Many Maltese have the unfortunate habit of shaking after their grooming sessions are complete, but a carefully made parting will help the hair fall back into place.

To avoid soiling the coat when the dog is eating, some Maltese owners like to attach bands at the sides of the face so that the hair does not fall into the food. Likewise, owners of show dogs sometimes band up the hair at the back of the hind legs to avoid coat soilage during potty visits.

CRACKERING

Also known as "wrapping," crackering is truly an art. If not done correctly, it can damage rather than improve the coat. It is essential to receive expert training from an experienced groomer before attempting to wrap the coat yourself.

In essence, crackering involves oiling the coat, then wrapping small sections of hair in paper or plastic, secured by an elastic band. Each packet needs to be opened every one or two days so that the coat can be brushed through before re-wrapping. You can see that this is a time-consuming task, only done by the truly dedicated Maltese enthusiast!

EARS AND EYES

The Maltese grows hair inside the ears, so it will be necessary to remove this carefully, either with blunt-ended tweezers or with your fingertips. If you remove just a few hairs at a time, this should be entirely painless.

Every dog's ears must be kept clean, and for this you may use a cotton ball or pad and a special ear cleaner, which will be in the form of a powder or liquid. Always take extreme care not to delve into the ear canal or you could

damage the ear.

If your dog has been shaking his head or scratching at his ears, there may well be an infection or ear mites. A thick brown discharge and

A part is drawn down the middle of the head to separate the hair into two sections for the double topknot.

A finished double topknot, secured with dental elastics.

Fastening the single topknot. You may wish to use elastics with small bows attached for a special finishing touch.

malodorous smell are also indicative of these problems, so veterinary consultation is needed right away.

It is also always necessary to keep the areas around the eyes clean. Any coat not groomed thoroughly around the eyes can contribute to a build-up of sticky discharge, which will need to be carefully removed. If allowed

to build up, this is not only uncomfortable for your Maltese but also can become abrasive to the eye. Pet shops sell suitable tear-stain removal formulas.

At any sign of injury to the eye, or if the eye turns blue, veterinary attention must be sought immediately. If an eye injury is dealt with quickly it can often be repaired; if neglected, a problem can lead to loss of sight.

NAILS

Nails must always be kept trimmed, but how frequently they need clipping depends very much on the surfaces upon which your dog walks.

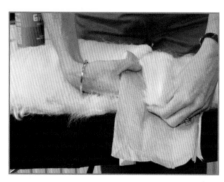

"Crackering" the coat is a time-consuming process to promote coat growth. The hair is conditioned and separated into sections, with a paper wrapper folded around each section.

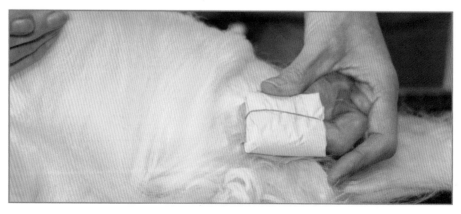

Each wrapped section is rolled up into a "packet" and secured with an elastic, as shown here.

Those living their lives primarily on carpets or on grass will need more frequent attention to their nails than those who regularly run or walk on hard surfaces.

Your Maltese should be trained to accept nail clipping from an early age, as it is especially important for this breed that long nails do not get caught in the coat. Take great care not to cut the quick, which is the blood vessel that runs through the nail, for this is painful. It is a good idea to keep a styptic pencil or some styptic powder on hand in case of an accident. Cutting just a small sliver of nail at a time is the safest approach.

ANAL GLANDS

A dog's anal glands are located on either side of the anal opening. Sometimes these become blocked and require evacuation. Experienced breeders often do this themselves, but pet owners would be well advised to leave this to their vets, for damage can be caused and evacuation is not always necessary.

GROOMING YOUR MALTESE

Overview

- Owning a Maltese means making a commitment to grooming throughout the dog's life.
- Show dogs must be kept in full coat. Pet owners can opt for the full coat or the clipped-down pet trim, the latter being more easily maintained but still requiring attention.
- Grooming is best done with the dog on a sturdy grooming table.
- Bathing is done as needed or as required by a dog's show schedule.
- Putting up the topknot is easy for the owner to learn; wrapping the coat, however, is an art that takes knowledge and practice.
- Grooming also includes care of the ears, eyes, nails and anal glands.

Keeping the Maltese Active

The best way to keep your Maltese active is to do things with him! All members of the family can engage your Maltese in fun games and playtime.

Although called a "toy," the Maltese enjoys leading an active lifestyle. Playing games with his owners helps to keep his intelligent mind alert, and he will enjoy this thoroughly. If two or more Maltese are kept together, they are sure to amuse themselves with their own games, much to the delight of their owners. Of course, a Maltese also appreciates a walk with his owner, for this is always a time for investigating new places and new smells, keeping his senses alert.

Most Maltese, when trained, are fairly obedient off lead, but you must always keep foremost in your mind that this is a very small breed, so accidents might just happen when they encounter larger, heavier dogs that they do not know. Those who keep their Maltese in long coat can still exercise them freely, but it is essential that all debris is removed from the coat after a run so that knots and tangles do not form. Because the coat of the Maltese is floor-length, it is also highly important that it is not left wet following exercise on damp ground. Obviously, if your Maltese is being actively exhibited in the show ring, this will be a main consideration when selecting your exercise area.

A Maltese kept as an only pet should ideally have at least one walk a day, but if he has other canine company and a large fenced yard in which to exercise, he may be happy

Give your Maltese some interesting toys and he will make up his own games.

A successful day in the ring! Dog showing is a popular pursuit among Maltese fanciers, whether participating or just attending to watch these silken-haired beauties glide around the ring.

CHAPTER 13

enough to go on outings less frequently.

A good number of Maltese are used in therapy work, visiting nursing homes and hospitals to meet and cheer up the residents there with a cuddle. The breed's convenient size and awe-inspiring loveliness make the visit something to which hospital patients and the elderly greatly look forward. It is also not unknown for a Maltese to become a "hearing dog" as an aid to the deaf. This is a dog that is especially trained to listen for sounds like telephones and doorbells ringing, something of great assistance to an owner with impaired hearing.

Some Maltese take part in

The Maltese's elegant confidence in the ring would make any handler happy to exhibit this naturally "showy" breed.

obedience trials and, being a highly active breed, they can enjoy taking part in agility trials, something that is great fun for both dogs and owners alike. It is delightful to see the tiny Maltese maneuvering his way over the little obstacles on the course. Fortunately, small breeds like the Maltese do not have to compete against larger ones like the Border Collie!

Even if your Maltese does not take part in any of these activities, you can enjoy endless hours of fun together. When not sleeping or relaxing, which the Maltese does with finesse, he will enjoy games with his suitably safe toys. Always remember, though, that toys should be checked regularly to ensure that no loose parts could cause accidental damage. Because the Maltese is a Toy breed with small teeth, toys designed specifically to be tugged are unsuitable for this breed.

KEEPING THE MALTESE ACTIVE

Overview

- The Maltese is a toy dog and much more than a lap dog. He enjoys being active with his owner.
- Games around the home and walks together are good ways to exercise the Maltese and spend time together bonding.
- Therapy work is a perfect job for the Maltese, whose beauty and sweet nature are sure to brighten anyone's day. He can also be trained for some assistance work.
- Being a toy dog does not exclude the Maltese from obedience and agility competition. His intelligence and energy enable him to succeed.
- Of course, your Maltese thoroughly enjoys quiet time, relaxing at home with his favorite people.

CHAPTER 14

Your Maltese and His Vet

One of the first things you and your pup will do together is visit the vet. The pup may or may not need vaccinations right away, but he will need a thorough check-up and an appointment to come back when it's time for his shots.

A visit to the vet can cause any dog to be rather apprehensive, added to which, unless going along just for a routine visit, your Maltese will probably be feeling a little "off color" at the time. To instill confidence, keep him on your lap in the waiting room and talk to him reassuringly to put him at his ease.

Your Maltese should always be well groomed, but if just visiting the vet for a check-up or vaccination, please be sure that your dog's coat is clean, as a courtesy to your vet. Obviously, if there is a crisis, waste no time in getting to the vet as a matter of urgency. Do not waste time with grooming; your vet will fully understand, and time may be at a premium.

It is sensible to make early contact with your vet, in part to build up rapport for any consequent visits. Obviously, if your puppy's course of vaccinations is not yet complete, you will need to take him to the vet in any case, but it is a good idea to take him for a thorough health check within the first few days of his coming home.

If you do not already have a vet for other family pets, you should select carefully. Preferably take recommendations from someone who has dogs of their own and whose opinion you trust. Location is also an important

A gorgeous Maltese coat does not "just happen." Coat quality is a direct reflection of overall good health, nutrition and care.

A good breeder makes sure her pups have the healthiest start in life by only breeding healthy, sound dogs that have tested free of genetic disorders.

factor, for you must be able to get your dog to the veterinarian quickly in an emergency, and the veterinarian must be able to respond rapidly when needed. If you live in a rural area, please be sure that you choose a veterinarian who has plenty of dealings with small animals, specifically Toy breeds. Many have a great deal of experience with farm animals but limited experience with dogs, as some dog owners have learned to their regret in the past.

VACCINATIONS

Routine vaccinations vary slightly depending on where

This mini-pack of Maltese enjoys each other's company. Some feel that dogs in multi-pet households are less prone to experiencing separation anxiety, since they always have a friend around.

you live and the type of vaccine used by your particular vet. Your veterinarian will advise you exactly about timing, when your dog can be exercised in public places after the course is complete and when boosters are due. Many vets now send reminder notices for boosters, but you should still make a note on your calendar so you're sure to keep your pup's appointments. If overdue, it will probably be necessary to give the full vaccination program again. If you are visiting your veterinarian for an initial vaccination program, do not allow your dog to

A healthy Maltese has a lustrous coat, a twinkle in his eye and an alert demeanor. You will know your Maltese well and should be able to detect any signals that he is feeling under the weather.

come into close contact with other dogs in the waiting room, nor indeed the waiting-room floor!

Some people prefer not to subject their animals to routine vaccinations, but opt for a homeopathic alternative. This needs to be carried out to the letter, so you must be guided be a veterinarian who also

Ticks can be especially difficult to detect on long-haired breeds like the Maltese.

practices homeopathy. Also bear in mind that it will probably be difficult to find a kennel that accepts a dog without proof of a routine conventional vaccination program.

PREVENTATIVE CARE

If your puppy has been bought from a truly dedicated breeder, all necessary care will have

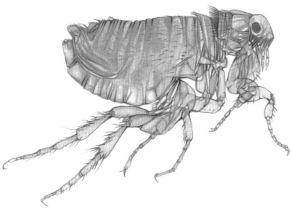

Today many reliable anti-flea products are available for use in routine healthcare.

been provided not only for the litter but also the dam. She will have had regular health checks and boosters, with a worming routine. These will stand her puppies in good stead and

provide them with greater immunity than would otherwise be the case.

It is also of great importance that any recommended tests for genetic abnormalities were carried out prior to the mating. Certainly, a genuinely caring breeder will in any case have bred only from a sound, healthy bitch and will have a selected a stud dog of similar quality.

CHECK-UPS

When your adult Maltese goes to the veterinarian annually for his booster vaccinations, your veterinarian will also give him a full physical exam. This will include a check of the heart, a dental exam and, if needed, a veterinary tooth cleaning. Blood may be drawn to run tests. The veterinarian also will check the dog's ears, nose, eyes, coat, skin, anal glands and so on. If you are grooming your Maltese regularly, you should be pretty confident that your dog's vital signs and body are normal, because you give him lots of hands-on attention. Of course, you will report any abnormalities to the vet.

NEUTERING AND SPAYING

Whether or not you decide to have your bitch spayed is a matter of personal choice, but it is something not to be undertaken without sufficient reason. In any event, please never allow a veterinarian to spay your bitch until after her first season. Timing "mid-season" will usually be advised.

Should you decide to opt for neutering your male dog or spaying your bitch, you will have to take special care with subsequent weight

Some considerations to make sure that your Maltese's time outdoors is safe and happy include protecting him from heatstroke, toxic plants, allergens and insects.

control by managing your dog's diet and exercise. In some cases, an aggressive or over-dominant male can be easier to cope with after neutering, but this is by no means always so.

Obviously there are some reasons of ill health that necessitate such operations, particularly pyometra, which will usually require a bitch's ovaries to be removed. In the case of a male with only one or neither testicle descended into the scrotum, your veterinarian may well advise castration to prevent the likelihood of cancer. Discuss all aspects of the procedure with your veterinarian.

YOUR MALTESE AND HIS VET

Overview

- Make your Maltese feel as comfortable as possible during trips to the vet.
- Select your veterinarian with care, taking recommendations if possible. Be sure you are satisfied with the clinic and the vet's experience with toy dogs.
- Your veterinarian will continue on where the breeder left off with the puppy's vaccinations.
- A Maltese pup gets the best start in life when bred from healthy parents.
- A healthy adult dog will visit the veterinarian annually for a thorough physical exam.
- Things to discuss with your veterinarian include parasite control and the pros and cons of neutering/spaying.
- Know your Maltese well so you'll recognize the signs of illness that tell you it's time to go to the veterinarian.